SALES LESSONS
from the
MASTERS

Frank Bettger

W. Clement Stone

Ben Feldman

Joe Gandolfo

KEN SMITH

SALES LESSONS FROM THE MASTERS

By Ken Smith

Copyright 2014

First Printing 2014.

Second Printing 2017.

Printed in the United States Of America.

ISBN 978-0-9845581-6-2

You can contact Ken at –
Ken@kensmithsales.com.
To leave thoughts and comments on book and application of sales principles, just go to kensmithsales.com. You can also sign up to receive Ken's blog with sales ideas and comment.

ACKNOWLEDGMENTS

I want to thank Bob Boyajian, president of Heartland LTC and former Senior Vice President of Combined Insurance, for sharing his experiences working with W. Clement Stone. In addition, I want to thank Marvin Feldman, president of Feldman Financial Group, for insights on his father, Ben Feldman — especially those insights related to packages and focus. As an industry, we should all thank Marvin for his contributions with the Life Happens program. I also want to thank all the regional sales managers, regional sales coordinators, product specialists and sales interns for being there to test the sales principles in this book and for being my test audience for stories. And I offer a very special thanks to my editor and friend, Chuck Hirsch. There are few writers who understand the audience in the life and health industry as well as Chuck.

Ken Smith

ABOUT THE AUTHOR

Ken Smith CLU is President of Ken Smith
Sales Training and Consulting, Inc. Ken has
35+ years of insurance experience in both field
and home office positions. Prior to starting
Ken Smith Sales Training and Consulting, Ken
was with Assurity Life for 12 years and prior
was with Mutual of Omaha for 11 years.
He was one of the organizers of the Critical
Illness Working Group and is a past president
of National Association for Critical Illness
Insurance. He is a member of the International
DI Society.

Ken has written numerous articles for
insurance industry publications, and has
conducted many presentations and training
sessions on sales techniques, critical illness and
disability income to a variety of audiences. His
usual audience is made up primarily of
producers and financial advisors. Ken has also
addressed the World Critical Illness Insurance
Conference, International DI Society, and
Society of Actuaries.

Ken understand firsthand the challenges of the sales profession.

He also writes and posts a weekly sales and motivational blog.

In addition to speaking, training and coaching, Ken works with clients to develop sales and marketing strategies.

FOREWORD

They say history repeats itself, and sometimes it is for the good and sometimes not so much. The sales principles presented here are timeless and worth repeating — daily. In his 1940 speech, "The Common Denominator of Success," Albert E. N. Gray said that one of the principles of successful people is that they form the habits that unsuccessful people are unwilling to do. Successful people have a purpose that is so strong that they are willing to do the activities to carry out their purpose. Frank Bettger, W. Clement Stone, Ben Feldman, and Joe Gandolfo are legends, champions, and icons. Yet, as important as they are, they are not the most important. The most important person today is you. You have the opportunity to learn from the best and then make the choice to apply the principles to capture the result. You are the person who will make the choice to carry on the legacy of these sales principles — enriching yourself and passing on the wisdom to others. In addition, because of your application of these sales principles, you will be positively serving others with your products and services.

Table of Contents

Chapter 1

Introduction

Several years ago, I was responsible for conducting a program called Critical Steps. Critical Steps is comprehensive training on selling critical illness protection. The sessions were two to four hours long, with only ten minutes of product training. In 2013, I presented approximately 60 to 70 sessions of Critical Steps training. The training was focused on the need for critical illness protection and on sales ideas and sales concepts. The basic sales ideas and concepts could be used with any insurance product -- life, income protection, long-term care, Health insurance, etc. The feedback from these sessions was incredible. New agents were excited because the focus was on sales ideas and concepts rather than on product. Long-time agents told me it has been years since they have had training like this.

The newer agents wanted more. The experienced agents told me, "Those are great ideas I used years ago. They worked so well. I don't know why I had stopped using them." In the training, I include specific sales principles from sales giants Frank Bettger and W. Clement Stone. The attendees' love Bettger's and Stone's ideas. One week, I conducted five training sessions including the state National Association of Insurance and Financial Advisors convention in Hawaii. After each of those meetings, Attendees told me that I needed to put this information into a book. Late in the fall of 2013, my friend Jeff Spain and I were discussing issues facing our industry. One of those issues was the lack of actual sales training. After talking with Jeff, I knew it was time to act.

Background

I have a question for you. What's the difference between plagiarism and research? Here's the Ken Smith answer, if you steal one idea it is plagiarism, but if you steal multiple ideas it is research. I admit to doing a lot of research through my career.

My heroes have always been great salespeople in the life and health insurance business. I still get excited when I meet a great salesperson. I can always learn something new. The greatest life insurance salesman ever, Ben Feldman said, only the fool learns from his experience. The wise man learns from the experience of others. When I started in the business, insurance sales were considered the major leagues of sales because the insurance agent doesn't sell anything tangible like a car or an appliance. Insurance agents sell ideas and concepts. Insurance salespeople were – and in my opinion still are -- the best of the best.

I hope you'll look at this book version as a collection of the greatest hits from some of the greatest salespersons ever in the life insurance business: Frank Bettger, W. Clement Stone, Ben Feldman, and Joe Gandolfo. It's an opportunity to learn from each of them.

I selected these four salespersons because of the impact and influence they have had on me. Those who know me personally, who have been through one of my training sessions, or who watch my video blogs will immediately recognize my sources. They very freely shared their ideas and wanted others to succeed. Today's world is dramatically different then the world in which they sold. Success and sales principles, however, do not change. I agree with W. Clement Stone that principles are like the laws of nature, they work 100% of the time. The law of gravity sates that if you drop an object from the roof of a building, it will drop to ground. It will happen 100% of the time. It will never go up. The same is true with sales and success principles. They are constant. My intent is to focus on principles.

The problem is today we are looking for fast answers. We have become blinded to the old principles that work and will always work.

Before we proceed any further, I have a few caveats.

First, my apologies to my female readers. Many of the quotes come from a time when there were few women in sales. Fortunately for all of us, there are more women in sales today.

Second, at one time, when most life insurance sales were whole life sales, volume was used to measure production. Volume equaled face amount. For example, if I sold a $100,000 whole life policy, then that was $100,000 in sales. Feldman's and Gandolfo's records are impressive today. Their records are even more impressive when you consider inflation and that, at the time they were selling, the cost per $1,000 of insurance was even more expensive than it is today.

And third, please note how I am presenting these ideas. Bettger, Stone, Feldman, and Gandolfo each have separate chapters. Each chapter focuses on the person and the unique sales ideas and principles related to that person. The last chapter focuses on common denominators that made these sales giants successful.

Expectations

Above all else, this book is about you. It's about you taking these specific sales ideas, more general sales concepts, and unchanging sales principles and putting them to use to help you become more successful.

I want you to write down the things you think of as a result of the principles and what I say. The exception is if you are driving wait till you stop. I don't want to be responsible for any accidents.

At the end of each chapter, write down those thoughts. Pick one idea and then focus on how you can implement that principle.

Chapter 2

Frank Bettger

"Set aside time to plan how you will spend your time. Think about what's most important. Then do those things first."
Frank Bettger

I was in my early 20s when I read Frank Bettger's book How I Raised Myself from Failure to Success in Selling for the first time. I could relate to the challenges Bettger wrote about as he began his career in the insurance business. I felt as though he was talking directly to me. He shared how his attending a class taught by Dale Carnegie himself helped turn his career around. As a result of reading about that, I signed up the next week for the Dale Carnegie course. The cost of that course was just about equal to what I earned in a month.

After rereading this book over the past several years, I now realize that his sales principles and concepts are timeless. And evidently, it's not just me who realizes that; check out the reviews for the book on Amazon.com. When I last checked, there were more over 600 recent reviews.

Think about it. Here's a book that Bettger published in 1947 that is still positively impacting salespeople today, 70 years later. Dale Carnegie said it was best book ever on selling. It kept me in the business that first year. Bettger's story is inspirational. He was born in 1888. His father died young, leaving his mother with five children to support. Bettger had to drop out of school after eighth grade to help support his family. He played baseball as a youngster, and he continued to do so, working his way to the major leagues with the St. Louis Cardinals until a shoulder injury ended his baseball career.

After baseball, he found a job riding a bicycle in Philadelphia, making collections. That's what he was doing when Fidelity Mutual Life Insurance Company recruited him, and he entered the insurance business. He was failing miserably in the life insurance business, but he was able to turn his career around. His turn-around became a great success story from which we can all learn.

As a result of his success selling life insurance, he traveled the United States conducting sales clinics with Dale Carnegie. In addition to How I Raised Myself from Failure to Success in Selling, he authored two other books: How I Multiplied my Income and Happiness in Selling and How I Learned the Secrets of Success in Selling. Bettger was also involved with the founding and development of the National Speakers Association.

Sales Principle 1: Sell with Enthusiasm

Today, enthusiasm is something you hear very few people talk about, but it is one of the most important qualities for success.

Bettger shared the story of when, as a young baseball player, he was released from a minor-league team because the manager thought he was lazy. He told the manager all he was doing was try to hide his nervousness.

At that point, Bettger made up his mind that he would never be called lazy again. He was able to get a job with another team and made up his mind to establish himself as the most enthusiastic player in his new league. After his first game with the new club, the local newspaper referred to him as Pep Bettger. Bettger writes that, when he acted enthusiastically, three things happened:

•   First, enthusiasm overcame his fear.
•   Second, his enthusiasm affected the other players, and they also became enthusiastic.
•   And third, he felt better after the game than he did before the game.

Bettger's enthusiasm carried him to the major leagues with the St. Louis Cardinals. A shoulder injury ended his baseball career, he found a job making collections for an installment furniture company. As he described it, one dollar down and the balance in "uneasy" multiple payments. After two years of collections, he started selling life insurance with Fidelity Mutual.

After ten months with Fidelity Mutual, Bettger was failing miserably selling life insurance and was already looking for another job. His sales manager told him that he wasn't cut out to be a salesperson and that he was cutting off his draw. Bettger realized that no matter what job he did, he would have to overcome his fears.

Bettger heard about a class that Dale Carnegie was holding, and he signed up for it. The first night, Dale Carnegie was talking about the power of enthusiasm. That Carnegie speech made Bettger think about his baseball career. The following morning Bettger convinced his sales manager to give him another 30 days. He committed himself to acting enthusiastically on every call.

How does this apply to you? Two questions for you: Are you making a conscious effort to put enthusiasm into your presentations? Are you enthusiastic in your presentation?

Bettger shares the story of a man he met who was selling patent medicine. Bettger described that stuff as being worthless, but Bettger noticed that the man was selling a lot of it because of his enthusiasm.
Bettger asked the man if he was always so enthusiastic.
The man told him, "Nah, I wasn't making expenses, but I noticed that when I put some punch into it, people started to buy."
The man noticed that sales increased and decreased with his personal level of enthusiasm.

We are all familiar with insurance salespeople who are great technical experts. They know products inside and out, but they hardly sell anything and, in time, fade from the business. One of the reasons for that, I believe, is a lack of enthusiasm.

The other side of that coin is the salesperson who lacks the technical skill but who succeeds because he or she is enthusiastic. Think about it. If you are enthusiastic, your listener is more likely to become enthusiastic even if you present your ideas poorly.

Bettger wrote that, in his years of selling, he saw enthusiasm double and triple the income of many salespeople, and he also saw hundreds fail because they lacked enthusiasm. He believed that enthusiasm is the biggest single factor in successful selling.

What will enthusiasm do you for? It will help you overcome fear -- which it did for Bettger, myself, and many others – you will become more successful in business, make more money, and enjoy a healthier, richer, and happier life.

Can merely acting enthusiastically change your life and sales? Yes! William James, the father of American psychology, said that feelings follow actions. If you want to be a certain way, all you have to do is act that way.

How do you become enthusiastic?

YOU ACT ENTHUSIASTICALLY!!!

I know this from personal experience! When I force myself to act enthusiastically, I feel enthusiastic.

Sales Principle 2: See the People

Bettger tells the story of how, at one point in time when he was out looking for other jobs, he was sneaking back into his office to pick up a couple of things. While he was there, the president of Fidelity Mutual came in to hold an impromptu meeting with the company's salespeople. Bettger was stuck; he couldn't sneak out.

He said the president said one thing that had a profound impact on his life: "Gentlemen, after all, this business of selling narrows down to one thing… seeing the people! Show me anyone who will tell his story to four or five people a day and I'll show you someone who can't help but do good."
The president had worked in every department and sold personally for several years, Bettger that he knew what he was talking about.

Bettger took him at his word and made up his mind that he was going to see five people a day. He also started keeping records of his calls.

During the following ten weeks, Bettger sold more than he had in the previous ten months. It proved to him that the president knew exactly what he was talking about. With today's technology, the way we meet with prospects has changed, the number of people to whom we present may change, but the importance of telling our story and seeing the people hasn't changed.

Bettger says that selling is the easiest job in the world if you work it hard – but the hardest job in the world if you work it easy. Take a minute and think about that statement.

You can't collect your commission until you make the sale. You can't make the sale until you write the order. You can't write the order until you have the interview. And you can't have the interview until you make the call!

The foundation of the business of selling – calls!

The more calls you make, the more you sell.

Bettger noticed that whenever sales fell off, he could narrow down the problem to one factor -- he wasn't seeing the people.

The number of calls and the way we make calls may change over time, but the principle itself has not changed. If you want to make sales, you have to make calls.

Sales Principle 3: The Secret of Leads and Prospecting

The number one issue in our business has always been prospecting. A top agent with another company once told Bettger, "Prospecting is selling. Getting leads is as important as getting applications, because when we stop getting leads, we stop getting applications."

Bettger asked him, "How do you get leads?" The answer was, ask for them! Just start asking for them, and you'll teach yourself. Ask everyone you try to sell -- even if you don't make a sale. Bettger always tried to get two names from everyone he called on.

After hearing about referred leads, Bettger went back to every person he had ever sold. He said he soon discovered how stupid he had been, letting every sale run into a dead end. He realized that he had been walking away from more business then he was selling when he didn't ask for referred leads.

Initially Bettger's referred leads were family members, wives, children, sisters, and in-laws of the person he just sold.

Was it hard at first? Yes. But as you teach yourself, Bettger wrote, it becomes a part of you and you do it automatically.

Sales Principle 4: The Secret to Sales – Questions

When Bettger says that asking questions is the secret to sales, he isn't just talking about asking any kind of questions. Instead, he means the secret is learning to ask the right questions.

Bettger tells of the time he attended a sales conference. The speaker talked about how, as a salesperson, he was failing because he was making too many positive statements. The speaker demonstrated that, rather than argue with his prospect, he would ask the prospect questions.

The key was, that when the prospect raised an objection, the salesperson asked questions that the prospect had to address. With this approach, the prospect would not get the impression that the salesperson was arguing with or contradicting him. The questions would lead to a sound conclusion based on facts. The salesperson was extremely forceful; yet never once did he argue, contradict, or offer a fixed opinion of his own.

Where else did Bettger learn the importance of asking questions? Socrates. Socrates' method was to ask questions, instead of telling people they were wrong. By a series of direct questions, Socrates would help the other person find the truth for himself. Frequently, the other person couldn't prove the truth of the things he believed.

It's also important to note that when you are asking questions you are helping your prospect clarify their thinking, and your prospect won't feel threatened. Questions get to the most important secret in sales, finding out what the other person wants and helping them get it. There are six important advantages you gain by asking questions:

1.   Asking questions helps avoid arguments.
2.   Asking questions helps you avoid talking too much.
3.   Asking questions enables you to help the other person recognize what he or she wants and helps him or her decide how to get it
4.   Asking questions helps the other person crystalize his or her thinking, and the idea you are discussing becomes his or her idea, not yours.
5.   Asking questions helps you find the most vulnerable point to close the sale. In other words, asking questions helps you get to the key issue faster.

6.   Asking questions gives the other person a feeling of importance because you are showing your respect for his or her opinion. As a result, your prospect will be more likely to respect you and your opinion.

I love Bettger's story of how he sold a large insurance policy to a New York manufacturer. Bettger tells of how he spent two hours preparing a list of 14 questions. When he arrived, the manufacturer had a stack of proposals from about ten different insurance companies. The manufacturer asked him to leave the proposal, and the manufacturer would make a decision the following week.
Bettger started asking his questions. He asked question after question, and in less than 45 minutes he and his prospect were on their way to have the manufacturer examined for the policy.

The combination of preparation and questions is magic.

One of Bettger's most powerful questions for a business owner is, "How did you start this business?" When the salesperson asks that question, two things happen – people love to talk about themselves so the business owner begins to open up, and the salesperson begins to gain tremendous insight into his or her wants and needs.

Bettger wrote about his three rules of selling, which all tie in to one another:

First, find out what the other person wants. Second, direct his or her conversations with questions that he or she will enjoy answering. Third, LISTEN.

Sales Principle 5: Planning and Study

Bettger read a Benjamin Franklin quote that only a few men live to an old age and even fewer become successful. As a result, Bettger started getting up an hour earlier every morning, and as he referred to it, he joined the "six o'clock club."

Bettger found the first hour to be the most exhilarating hour of his day. His mind was clear and his house was quiet.

Bettger would spend 30 minutes of the hour studying and reading about life insurance and tax issues. As a result of his increasing knowledge, he began to gain confidence with regard to calling on businesses. For the other half hour, he planned his day, thought about his calls for the day, said a silent prayer for enthusiasm, and if he had any time left over, read an inspirational magazine.

If you want to grow in business, you have to make time to study and grow.

As Henry Ford said, "Anyone who stops learning is old – whether at 20 or 80. Anyone who keeps learning stays young. The greatest thing in life is to keep your mind young."

Bettger also set aside Saturday mornings as his "self-organization day." He used the time to go over records, study calls, plan exactly what he would say to each person, and arrange each day's calls for the following week. As a result, on Monday morning, instead of having to force himself to make calls, he made his calls with confidence and enthusiasm.

Bettger was eager and well-prepared to see prospects, because he had thought about them, studied their situations, and had ideas that he believed might be of value to them. He said that at the end of the week, instead of feeling exhausted and discouraged, he felt exhilarated, knowing that following week would be even better.

Sales Principle 6: Sell Yourself

You can't sell something you don't believe in yourself.

You need to sell yourself first. If you haven't sold yourself, how can you answer the most common objection: "I can't afford it!"? That's a pretty tough objection to overcome if you feel that way yourself.

Bettger was talking with some successful producers and found that every one of them was enthusiastic about their personal life insurance programs. They were excited about the amount of life insurance they owned. He found they all increased their programs first and then worked like hell to pay for them.

At the time, Bettger owned a $1,000 policy. He filled out an application for $25,000. He determined that all he had to do to pay for the new policy was to increase his own production by $50,000 over the year --only $1,000 more a week.

After increasing his personal life insurance, Bettger jumped from ranking 92nd in the company sales production standings to 13th within the following year. He said he no longer feared the objection, "I can't afford it!" He said he was able to look his prospect straight in the eye and respond with confidence.
After he sold himself, Bettger began to sell like never before.

Sales Principle 7 -- Stories Sell

One of the many valuable ideas I have learned from Bettger is that stories sell. Anyone who works with me or has been through one of my training sessions will attest that stories are part of me.

Selling is, in a sense, storytelling: the salesperson is telling a story about what he or she is selling. The salesperson is putting ideas into action. Stories dramatize ideas and concepts.

Bettger's books are great examples of using stories to illustrate a point and to motivate. He believed that stories were vital factors in his success.

If the salesperson's sales story gives the listener an idea that will make him or her money or solve some problems, he or she will get excited and will want to do business with that salesperson.

A successful agent who once worked with Bettger said, "I kept wondering when you were going to stop telling stories and start selling – all the time the sale was being made and I didn't even know it!"

The key here is that the story must relate directly to the prospect's problem.

How does the salesperson learn to tell stories well? By telling stories. After the salesperson has told a story a few times, her or she will find himself or herself improving each time it's told. The salesperson will learn to eliminate all the needless words and details. The salesperson will be excited!

Frank Bettger's Sales Principles

To summarize, Frank Bettger built a tremendous sales career on seven solid sales principles.

1. Sell with Enthusiasm
2. See the People
3. The Secret of Leads and Prospecting
4. The Secret to Sales – Questions
5. Planning and Study
6. Sell Yourself
7. Stories Sell

The salesperson who is looking to grow professionally would do well to ask himself or herself, "Where might my own career go if I applied these same principles to my personal sales efforts?"

Chapter 3

W. Clement Stone

"You can evaluate the principles I'm sharing with you by one standard only: the action you take and results you achieve." -- W. Clement Stone

W. Clement Stone was born in Chicago, Illinois. His father died when Stone was three years old. His mother was a dressmaker. She moved to Detroit and purchased an insurance agency. There, at age 16, he started selling accident insurance. He learned to make cold calls going from office to office.

Stone returned to Chicago at age 20. He established Combined Registry Company and began selling pre-issue accident plans. When an agent sold these kinds of plans, the agent would fill in and obtain information from the prospect, then tear off and hand the policy to the prospect at the time of the sale. It was instant issue 100 years ago.

Through trial and success, Stone developed a sales system for selling a large number of accident policies. He then started personally recruiting agents shortly after establishing his agency.

The depression hit. His agents' sales declined. Then it hit him that he had not even been bothering to see his salespersons and sales managers; in a sense, he had recruited them and then left them on their own.

After realizing how he had let his sales team down, Stone started working with them personally and sending them sales ideas on a regular basis. His goal was to train both his current and new salespersons so that they would do as well or better than him.

In 1937, Stone read Napoleon Hill's Think & Grow Rich, and the book changed him and his sales team. He required all of his salespeople to read the book. As a result, sales managers became leaders of super salespeople, and his salespeople began to set sales records.

By 1939, Stone's agency represented a large eastern accident and health company. He had more than 1,000 full time agents, and his agency had representation in every state. It's hard to imagine, but his contract with the carrier was a verbal contract. One day, while on vacation, he received notice from the company that it intended to terminate the arrangement.

Stone was able to convince the carrier not to terminate the contract. But as a result of the uncertainty that discussion created, he set a goal for himself that he would organize his own life and health insurance company, and that by 1956 it would be the largest in the United States. He met that goal -- in 1956, Combined Insurance was the largest company exclusively writing accident and health insurance business.

In 1952, Stone convinced Napoleon Hill to come out of retirement. The two formed a partnership that lead to the writing of Principles of Success Course and Success through a Positive Mental Attitude. Stone also wrote The Success System that Never Fails.

While writing his books, Stone had to find a way to write without sacrificing time from his company. He slept only a few hours a night and hired two additional secretaries. The secretaries would work in shifts, and when the last secretary left for the day, Stone would continue working using a Dictaphone. Remember, in those days, there weren't word processors, let alone personal computers.

By the 1950s, every insurance agency and company that sold pre-issue accident policies had discontinued sales, with one exception – Stone's companies. Because he had developed a sales system, he and his salespeople were able to sell more policies in a week than other salespeople sold in a month.

One of the reasons for Stone's success was that he focused and concentrated on a single kind of policy, and all of the attention focused on that policy's sale.

Even into his 80s, Stone would go to bed at 1:00 am and get up at 5:45 am. He always took a 30-minute nap at noon. He said that the nap made him feel like he was starting a new day.

Stone's goal was to change the world. He did it both with his financial contributions and with his impact on people, personally and through his writing. Stone succeeded in making the world a better place.

It's telling to realize that Stone has been gone from active management of Combined Insurance for more than 25 years, yet employees still refer to him as Mr. Stone out of respect.

Sales Principle 1: Attitude

For W. Clement Stone, the first and most important secret of successful insurance sales is that there are no secrets; sales success starts with a positive mental attitude.

Sales are contingent upon the attitude of the salesperson – not the attitude of the prospect.

I believe that statement was a foundational key to Stone's success. He believed that the salesperson who is inspired and has the proper "know how" and knowledge can influence the prospect to buy.

I must admit, I used to have my doubts about this principle. You may have doubts too, but before you decide, consider the following examples from Stone.

During the depression, he had an arrangement with Commercial Casualty to issue a new policy. His sales managers said it couldn't be sold. His salespeople tried to sell it, and they said the premium was too high.

That summer, for 10 weeks, he personally sold the policy. Because Stone sold it successfully, his salespeople were motivated to try. As a result of Stone's personal sales, they found it to be just as easy to sell as the company's other plans.

Here's another example. Stone was working with a salesperson who was complaining about not making any sales in Sioux Center, Iowa. The salesperson complained that it was impossible for him to sell people who were Holland Dutch because they were clannish and there had been recent crop failures that had depressed the area. Stone told him that the following day they were going back to Sioux Center. Stone said, "I'll sell most of the day, and you can sell for an hour or two."

Stone told the salesperson, "Success is achieved by those who try, and maintained by those who keep trying with a positive mental attitude. There is an intelligent solution to any problem, if you keep your mind on what you want and off what you don't want."

Stone conditioned his mind in this way. He told himself, "So, the Holland Dutch are clannish, and therefore they won't buy. That's wonderful! What's so wonderful about it? It's a well-known fact that if you can sell to one of the clan, you can sell to the entire clan. All you have to do is make the first sale. This can and will be done. The Holland Dutch are marvelous people. They are responsible and want to protect their families, and haven't purchased accident insurance from any other salesperson. Our policies offer excellent protection at a low cost. Therefore, they are just waiting for me. I have no competition."

Beginning with the bank, Stone began to sell store after store, and office after office. Other than one of the bank tellers, Stone sold everyone. The salesperson took over at the end of the day, and he sold everyone as well.

As part of my company's Critical Steps Training, I share the following example:

A young salesperson just starting out asked Stone for the names of Stone's friends, and he asked Stone whether he could use Stone's name when he called. Stone told him, "No problem. Come by tomorrow and my secretary will have some cards with names, addresses, and telephone numbers."

The salesperson picked up the cards and then came back to Stone's office on Friday, excited. He told Stone that he had sold eight out of the ten and had appointments with the other two. He asked Stone whether Stone could give him more names. Stone said, "I am kind of busy right now. Here's the telephone book. When I gave you that first list, all I did was pick out one name from the As, another from the Bs, another from the Cs, and so on."

The prospects whom the salesman called on had no idea who Mr. Stone was, but because the salesperson believed they were friends of Mr. Stone, he got appointments and made sales.

What do you think? Are sales contingent on the salesperson or the prospect?

Sales Principle 2: Planning and Study

One of the most important habits the salesperson can develop is taking time near the end of each day to plan the next day's activity. This stimulates thinking about goals and studying how planned activities for the next day can carry the salesperson forward.

As Stone points out, this planning activity helps "program" the salesperson's mental computer. The subconscious mind goes to work. Moreover, the salesperson "wakes up each day employed!"

Stone continuously emphasized to his management team the importance of setting aside thinking and planning time.

Sales Principle 3: A Solid Presentation

An organized presentation spells success.

Here are Stone's nine essential ingredients to a successful presentation. I will present these much as Stone himself would, in direct, "instructional" manner. In parenthesis, I have included lines from the Combined Insurance presentation:

1.   Use a good introduction. Everything must have a beginning. The purpose of the introduction is to get the prospect to listen and to arouse interest. (This will interest you also.)
2.   Concentrate the prospect's attention: Actually, look over the literature yourself while pointing to the illustration, thus using directional force of your own eyes to get the prospect to look at what you are pointing at. (Taught salesperson to use pen to point to policy to keep prospects attention and to look into prospects eyes when they wanted to make a point.)

3.   Relieve tension: You want your prospect to like you, so smile. If you can get prospects to laugh at effective humor, you can relieve tension with the prospect as well as neutralize timidity on your part. (Salesperson had standard joke. Mr. Prospect, we pay even if your feelings are hurt. It was corny but everyone laughed. It was more to relax the salesperson.)

4.   Use enthusiasm – if you talk in a sincere, enthusiastic manner, you will appeal to your prospects' emotions and accelerate your own enthusiasm.

5.   Ask questions. You can direct your prospects mind in a desired channel by asking specific questions that require answers other than a "yes or no" reflex answer. You want a series of "yes" answers; ask questions that make it easy for your prospect to answer yes. (Asked a series of questions to direct the prospect's mind.)

6.   Give the complete description. Explain the full advantage of the product. If time is short, use as few words as possible.

7.   Use influential names. Persons buy what people buy, and people buy what other persons buy. The use of influential names reduces sales resistance. (Show the names of people who have already purchased from you.)

8.   Show something – brochures, pictures, illustrations, or visual aids -- that clearly create the picture in the prospect's mind.

9.   Use an effective close. Everything must have an ending. Agents who are not in large income brackets are generally those who do not close. (If you don't mind, I would like to write this for you? May I? Mr. Jones, what's your first name?)

No matter how long a show plays on Broadway, the actors continue to rehearse. They are professionals and continuously seek perfection. They know exactly what they are saying. They understand the response and reaction from their audience.

Stone looked at sales presentations much like an actor looks at his performance. He could put feeling, emotion, and timing into his memorized talk. When a person goes to the theater and sees a great actor, it seldom occurs to him or her that someone else wrote those lines. The theatre-goer may not realize that the actor's actions as well as his words are the same at every performance. The actor lives the part. And like a good playwright, the actor improves it at every opportunity. Unlike the playwright, Stone changed the talk to meet the changing conditions, but what he said became standardized for such occasions. Thus, if Stone was interrupted in the beginning of a presentation, he would use a standard joke to relieve tension rather than later in the latter part of the presentation. Other than that, Stone and the agents of Combined Insurance stayed with and followed the company presentation word for word.

Stone believed questions were an important part of selling. The philosopher Socrates had an effective system in the art of asking questions. Great salespeople use his method: Ask a question or a series of questions to which the prospect will readily agree, then ask concluding questions based on those agreements. This technique enables the salesperson to force a desirable response without seeming aggressive.

The sales person has to believe what he or she is doing. When he or she is convinced that what he or she is recommending is the best and most logical course of action for the prospect to take, the salesperson's mind is clear. It gives the salesperson confidence that nothing he or she encounters will become a deterrent.

During the presentation, the salesperson must speak the prospect's language — that means stay away from industry jargon.

The salesperson should simplify suggestions; the power of the salesperson's recommendations will lie in their simplicity. And simplicity always lies in comprehensive knowledge and thorough preparation.

The salesperson must speak as one who has authority. He or she must show enthusiasm for any suggestions he or she makes. Human emotions are highly transferable. The salesperson must look and speak in terms of success. Prospects buy from agents they perceive as being successful.

Clear, simple language carries the most conviction. The salesperson wants the prospect to fully understand all recommendations and feel that he or she has made the buying decision.

The presentation must include repetition. Repetition overcomes communication difficulties. The salesperson must try to make his or her meaning clear by furnishing examples and making analogies. Repeated assertion is hard to resist. The initial reaction of the human mind is to reject anything new. If the salesperson repeats something over and over, however, the prospect's natural defenses tend to weaken because the new idea is no longer new.

Sales Principle 4: A Success System

Stone's success was built on selling an accident policy. Stone would give his prospect the choice of one or two units. Nearly everyone purchased two units. His salespeople's objectives were to sell 20 policies a day or 100 a week.

If a salesperson made 20 presentations a day, he or she should have made that 20-sale goal, because he was making presentations to multiple people within a company or family.

And remember, his sales force focused only on the accident policy.

Stone was a great believer in the importance of the use of repetition in training as well as in selling. Repetition is critical in training, especially when learning something new. I have said that one of my goals in life is to repeat the same message to an agent eight times in slightly different ways. Then he or she will call and say, "Ken, I have this great idea," and it's my words coming back to me.

I have learned a lot from W. Clement Stone, but the most valuable is the use of repetition in both training and learning.

Stone believed that it takes less work to succeed than to fail. It also takes less time to achieve success when the salesperson concentrates thoughts and effort on learning a lot about a little and becoming an expert, as opposed to disrupting energies by trying to learn a little about a lot. Therefore, the salesperson must focus his or her attention and effort to acquire the necessary knowledge, "know how," and motivation to become an expert and achieve his or her desired objective.

At one time, many companies sold pre-issue accident policies on a cold canvas basis. By the 1950s, Stone's company was the only one still selling the policies. This was because he had developed a sales system, and he was able to sell more policies in a week than other salespeople sold in a month.

Stone was able to succeed in the long run because the company's efforts were concentrated on one policy, and attention was focused on its sale. He developed sales presentations and answers to all objections. His sales team learned his presentation word for word.

Later on, Stone added new benefits and new policies, such as sickness benefits, hospital indemnity, and life insurance. A separate sales force was created to sell each product. It was not unusual for someone from Combined Insurance to call on a policyholder every six months.

When sales reps went into a town, they first called on the mayor or police chief to make their first sale. Then, as part of the presentation, they would tell everyone that the mayor and police chief had purchased. The purchase by the mayor or police chief became a built-in testimonial for the town. The sales reps would go business to business, door to door, calling on everyone.

Motivation was an important part of Stone's success system.

Stone believed that success and sales principles are like laws of nature; they don't change. For example, the law of gravity -- what goes up must come down, and if you jump off buildings, you crash to the ground. It's the same way with success principles; they work 100% of the time. The salesperson is guaranteed success if he or she follows the principles. But the salesperson may never have a successful career nor achieve the desired objectives if he or she is ignorant of the principles or fails to use them.

Sales Principle 5: Emotions are Subject to Action

One of the most important principles for Stone is that emotions are subject to action, not reason. As I discussed in the chapter on Frank Bettger, if the salesperson acts enthusiastically, the salesperson will be enthusiastic. Try it for yourself.

Stone believed that the single most important factor in selling is enthusiasm. For years, when speaking to groups, he would have them stand up and say, "To be enthusiastic, you act enthusiastic."

In later years, he would ask the group, "How do you feel?"

The response would be, "I feel healthy! I feel happy! I feel terrific!"

When business starts to level off for a salesperson, he or she might start a new trend with new life, new blood, and new activities. But the salesperson must not abandon the successful formulas of the past and exchange them for new concepts. Why? Successful individuals, corporations, and nations subsequently fail from lack of attention to attitude and the PMA (Positive Mental Attitude) motivational principles that made them great in the first place.

The Combined Insurance sales team would meet every morning. Sales managers would provide motivation, the sales team would discuss goals for the day, and everyone would get fired up to make calls.

I talked with Stanley Beyer, former president of Pennsylvania Life Insurance Company and a person who in his own right is one of the greatest salespeople of his time. Stanley developed a success system with Pennsylvania Life. When talking with Stanley, I mentioned that some of the former Pennsylvania Life agents still meet in the morning, noon, and end of the day. After meeting in the morning and noon, they go out and make calls.

Stanley gave me some incredible insight. He said that people are bombarded with all kinds of negative thoughts and need to change their self-image. The agent has to learn to control his or her thoughts. That's why the salesperson needs the team and why the team meets in the morning, noon, and end of the day. This way, the salesperson can control his or her thoughts from breakfast to noon, then the salesperson needs the leader and the rest of the team members to help him or her refocus.

Bob Boyajian, a senior vice president at Combined who worked with Stone for about 30 years, told me that Stone cared deeply about his people. His door was always open and anyone could come in and talk about financial problems, marital problems, etc.

Bob said that Stone told the following story, which also appears in Stone's and Napoleon Hill's book, Success through a Positive Mental Attitude. A minister was watching his son while trying to work on an upcoming sermon. The minister needed to find a way to keep his son busy. The minister saw a map of the world in the newspaper, and he cut it up and gave it to his son. The minster told his son that he would pay him to put the map back together. The minister thought that would keep him busy for a long time.

A few minutes later, the son was back with the map together. The minister asked, "How did you do that so quickly?"

The son said, "There was a picture of a man on the other side."

The minister had a theme for his sermon: "If a man is right, his world is right."

Stone believed that if a man's world was right, the man's company also would be right.

Sales Principle 6: Goals are Important

When the salesperson knows what his or her goal is, several good things happen:

1.   The subconscious goes to work, following the universal law that "What the mind can conceive and believe, it can achieve." Because the salesperson visualizes his or her intended destination, his or her subconscious is affected by this self-suggestion and seeks ideas and solutions to help the salesperson get there.
2.   Because the salesperson knows what he or she wants, the salesperson recognizes opportunities that will help attain it. The salesperson gets on track. The salesperson gets into action.
3.   Work becomes fun. The salesperson is motivated to pay the price. The salesperson studies, thinks, and plans.

The more the salesperson thinks about his or her goal, the more enthusiastic the salesperson becomes. And with enthusiasm, desire turns into a burning desire.

Sales Principle 7: Self-Motivation

Stone used and taught self-suggestion to his sales reps. His methods were based on the work of French psychologist Emile Coué. Dr. Coué discovered that he could improve a patient's healing by having them repeat over and over the phrase, "Every day in every way, I'm getting better and better."

Stone extended this concept. He first used the concept to avoid procrastination. He would repeat, "Do it now!"
When a salesperson was hesitant about making a call, Stone's favorite comment was, "If there is nothing to lose and everything to gain, then by all means do it."
And then to avoid procrastination, Stone would add: "Do it now!"

W. Clement Stone's Sales Principles

To summarize, W. Clement Stone built a kind of insurance empire on seven solid sales principles that he both practiced and taught his company's sales force.

1. Attitude
2. Planning and Study
3. A Solid Presentation
4. A Success System
5. Emotions are Subject to Action
6. Goals are Important
7. Self-Motivation

No matter the experience level, the salesperson who is looking to increase sales will find a way to integrate these principles into his or her approach to the business.

Chapter 4

Ben Feldman

One of my favorite quote from Ben Feldman is "Only a fool learns from his own experience. The wise man learns from the experiences of others." That quote is the basis for this book. Ben Feldman is remembered by many as the greatest life insurance salesperson ever. Feldman started his insurance career in 1938 making $35 a week as a debit agent, which meant he literally went door to door selling insurance and collecting premiums. By 1941, he was the top agent in his company, earning $105 a week. He was selling $500 life insurance policies – and that was the death benefit.

Feldman said that, with a debit, the agent spends most of his or her time collecting, and then only if the agent has some time left over does he or she actually sell life insurance. He hated collecting and loved selling.

Feldman joined New York Life Insurance Company in 1942. That first year, he placed 168 policies with a total death benefit of $252,128. By 1944, he had doubled his production and placed $500,000 in 12 months. Feldman first qualified for the Million Dollar Round Table (MDRT) in 1945 with $1.1 million.

In 1956, he did $10,000,000 in life sales. With that, he was the first person to ever sell $10 million in a single year. In 1960, he sold $20,000,000. In 1966, sold $50,000,000. In 1969, he reached $100,000,000 and surpassed that benchmark regularly until his death in 1993. For perspective, consider that $100,000,000 in 1969 is approximately $680,000,000 in 2014 dollars, and 80% of his production was in whole life sales.

When Feldman was introduced at the MDRT Annual Meeting in 1981, there were still approximately 1,800 life insurance companies operating in the United States. It was estimated that he personally had more life insurance in force than two-thirds of those companies.

Feldman accomplished all this from East Liverpool, Ohio. He did business in East Liverpool, a town with a population of 20,000, and Youngstown, a town with a population of 175,000 about 40 minutes from East Liverpool. He knew every business owner in the area.

Here's a fact I love: His total volume exceeded $1.8 billion and he generated one third of that total after he was 65 years old!
In 1992, New York Life celebrated Feldman's 50th anniversary by promoting a sales contest during "Feldman's February." Guess who won? Eighty-year-old Ben Feldman!

I recommend the audio of "An Afternoon with Ben Feldman," which is available from the MDRT. I have shared this audio with a number of younger people in the life insurance business, and they always seem to find it of real value. Seth Groff, Assurity's life product manager, listened to it on a drive from Nebraska to Colorado. During the trip, he kept stopping to text me to let me know how much he loved Feldman's great ideas.

Feldman wrote two books, Creative Selling for the Seventies and Creative Selling for the 1990's. Both are out of print, but I was able to find used copies on Amazon.com.

Another related book I would also recommend is The Feldman Method by Andrew Thomson, who was Feldman's manager with New York Life.

Feldman was a person who measured success not by material standards, but by his influence on others – most specifically his influence for good, not just among his peers in the life insurance business, but also among the people his peers serve.

Sales Principle 1: Making Calls

At 1981 MDRT Annual Meeting, Feldman told his audience that there is no easy way to sell life insurance. But the key to making sales is simple – just make calls. Nothing happens until you make a call.

Feldman talked about the importance of momentum. For example, it's Monday. You make some calls and nothing happens. It was a lousy day. The same thing happens on Tuesday. You keep on making calls, and by the end of the week you may have made one sale. And you may have had a couple of call backs. The agent does it again the second and third weeks. In spite of people saying, "No," you keep at it.

You are beginning to build momentum. If you keep making the calls, you will start to make sales.

What you can't let happen after you start hearing people say "No," is to start making excuses and then quit making calls. Everything stops when you stop making calls. Just make the calls and sales will follow.

Sales Principle 2: Packages

For many years, I didn't realize that one of Feldman's keys to success was his ability to transform ideas and to package those ideas. Until I started researching his approach for this book, I never realized the importance of the packages in his sales success.

Likewise, over the years, I believe that many producers have been so focused on how much life insurance Feldman sold and to whom he sold, that they have missed the importance of packages in his success!

Feldman designed these packages to solve specific problems. Most often, these packages solved the prospects' fundamental need for cash.

The packages were always about what the product could do. Not what it is! He designed them to help take an idea that could be difficult to understand and simplify that concept so that almost anyone could understand. In short, a Feldman package painted a picture identifying the problem and solution without all the technical jargon.

For Feldman, the key to packaging an idea was to make it simple. The simpler the better. Each package solved a problem. All of his packages were blocks of whole life designed to solve specific problems for the prospect.

One package might be an educational package: "You want to be sure your daughter goes to college. May I show you this idea?" Or he might present a retirement package: "How would you like to retire with a guaranteed income for the rest of your life?"

Feldman sometimes used a "grandparents plan," designed to take advantage of gifting. He had various packages like, a "discount your tax" package, and a package he designed for partners that he called "a see-saw policy" – if one partner gets off, the other falls without life insurance protection. Which simply was life insurance to fund buy sell agreement.

Each package points out the prospect's need for life insurance in such a way that the prospect has to do something about it.

Some of Feldman's ideas for packages came from articles in magazines. Others came from talking with people, and others came from life insurance industry meetings.

Feldman would test the package concepts on his wife, kids, and people in his office. His son Marvin told me that he and his brother Richard knew a lot about life insurance before they graduated from high school, from their Dad testing the packages on them. Ben Feldman wanted his packages to be understood by a high school student. If package was simple enough for high school student to understand then a business owner should understand.

My question for you, would a high school student understand your presentation?

Marv told me that when his father finalized a package, he would have his secretary type it on 3x5 cards. He would post it on the corkboards in his office and start making calls.

After putting together, a new package, Feldman would make up a list of names and then start making his calls. The new package would excite him. When a package got old, he would work on a new one.

Another key to his packages was that they had to prove to his prospect that not solving this particular problem had a price tag on it, and that it would cost more to do nothing than to do something about it.

Thinking about Feldman's sales packages was an eye-opener for me. As many times as I have listened to him, it never hit me until recently what a sales package can do.

We all pick up ideas and concepts that work successfully, and then over time we stop using them. I have heard many agents tell me about a sales concept or idea that worked so well that he or she stopped using it. What happens in situations like that? We get bored. There's an insight we can gain from Feldman when that happens — we can create a new package.

Keep your presentations simple -- not only for the prospect's benefit, but for yours. If your presentation is simple, you'll be able to present it more effectively because you'll understand it inside and out.

Every person has a problem that only life insurance can solve. In the typical young man's case, the problem is to create cash. For the older person, the problem is usually to conserve cash. There are many variations on these problems. There are many ways to create plans to solve the problems as well.

For you, the challenge is to generate ideas of packages you can develop.

Sales Principle 3: Don't Sell Life Insurance!

Feldman believed that he didn't sell life insurance; he sold what life insurance does! In 2015, people in the United States bought 20 million one-quarter inch drill bits. But not a single person wanted a drill bit. What the buyers really wanted were one-quarter inch holes! They had to buy the drill bit to get the hole. The problem is that they need a hole. The solution is buying drill bits to make the hole.

One of the most important lessons I have learned from Feldman is that it's not about the product. It's about what the product does. But what do most people and companies in the life insurance business sell? The drill bits. Most industry training is focused on the product. There is very little discussion about what the product does. As a result, what do agents sell? The product!

Feldman never sold life insurance. Instead, he helped the prospect see that he or she had a problem and life insurance was the solution.

My question is, are you focused on the product or the solution to your prospect's problems?

Sales Principle 4: Simple Concepts

For me, listening to Ben Feldman explain the concept of life insurance is like listening to music that you love. Here's how he described it:

"When someone buys a life insurance policy, we put the face amount in escrow. That amount wasn't accumulated. It was created for the policy holder. You know most people create their money by accumulation–accumulating it slowly, painfully, over the years. But our job is not to accumulate but create. What do we create? Dollars that underwrite time.

"The basic purpose of life insurance is to create cash: Nothing more, nothing less. Everything else confuses the issue. Your job as a life insurance agent is to do what no one else can do. Do you know anyone else who can create money?"

Feldman carried a thousand-dollar bill in his case. He would open it up and the prospect would say, "What's that?"

Feldman would say, "That's what I sell, how many do you want?"

One time at a seminar, Feldman was asked, "What do you say when a prospect tells you he or she intends to buy term and invest the difference?"

Feldman responded, "Term insurance is temporary insurance. But, the problem? The problem is permanent."

Ask yourself, how would you respond to that question? Notice, Feldman offered no long dissertation, but a simple, confident response that comes from understanding, preparation, and study.

Sales Principle 5: Discounted Dollars

Ben would tell prospects, "Give me two cents, and I'll give you a dollar. I'll put the dollar in escrow. I'll write your name on it. I'll keep it in escrow for a year. If anything happens to you, we'll trade. I'll keep the two cents, and you get the dollar. And at the end of the year, if nothing happens to you, I'll repeat the offer. One dollar for another two cents. And I'll repeat the offer year after year."

At two cents a year, it takes a long time to pay a dollar for dollar, doesn't it? Know what kind of dollars the life insurance purchaser is buying? He or she is buying discounted dollars.

The two cents is the premium. And when are those discounted dollars delivered? Exactly when the buyer needs them -- when time has run out, when there is no more time to complete the buyer's plan. And those discounted dollars are tax-free.

You are selling is a contract that guarantees the delivery of tax-free dollars at a discount.

Sales Principle 6: Cash Value Life Insurance

Feldman would emphasize that saving money requires a system. A person has to build systems into a savings plan or there won't be any savings.

Statistics show that people save money for a little while. The average length of savings time will last about three years. Then the average person takes it out, spends it, and it's gone. Then the average person starts over, and same thing happens again. A week is gone; then a year is gone; now the person is 40 or 45; now he or she is 50; and then he or she is 60. Far too often, the person grows old and never saves any money.

This isn't because the person didn't make money. It's because the person didn't save it systematically.

The premium statement that the life insurance company sends the client can create that system I mentioned above. The client sends a few hundred dollars a month, and soon he or she has accumulated some money.

I know of people who don't know how much equity they have in life insurance. They never pay any attention to it. Point out to people how cash value life insurance can help people accumulate cash. It's there if the client needs it. Face value is in escrow. The cash value is there today. What you are doing by selling whole life insurance is helping a lot of people help themselves.

Sales Principle 7: Put Premiums into Perspective

Feldman always believed that paying the premium isn't the problem. Paying is the solution. Think about that statement, and it can completely change your attitude and perspective about the challenges of selling.

You must help prospects find the money. If you have pinpointed a problem and identified the solution, and the prospect is sold in principle, there still is no sale until the prospect pays the money for the premium.

Our job as agents is to help the prospect find the money.

The prospect doesn't need more money. The money is already there. Your job is to work through the prospect's priorities with the prospect in order to find the money.

You have to help the prospect put premiums into perspective. For example, Feldman would explain to a physician that the cost of the physician's retirement plan was one patient visit per day.

I once met an agent who worked with donut store franchisees. He would explain to the owners that the cost of his program was five minutes of sales between 7:00 and 7:05 every morning.

If someone asks me how much a critical illness plan costs, my response is always, "About a cup of coffee a day. For a younger person, it's a convenience store coffee a day. For someone more my age who uses tobacco, it's a giant Frappuccino at Starbucks."

If you have worked with me, you know that any illustration I have worked breaks down premiums on daily cost basis. Which is the reason I like using a cup of coffee Snacks or pop-- or whatever the prospect can relate to – as the comparison.

If you ask early in the interview, "What do you spend on snacks or coffee each day?" the prospect's response can help put premiums into perspective. By doing so, you minimize the cost in the mind of the prospect.

For example, prospect states they spend $5 a day on coffee and daily cost of insurance plan is $4.50. You respond that cost is less than you are spending and you will not have to change your lifestyle as a result.

Sales Principle 8: Sell Yourself

Throughout Feldman's career, he continued to buy more life insurance on himself. When he presented to the MDRT Annual Meeting in 1981, he owned $6 million dollars of participating whole life and was paying $7,500 in premiums a week.

If you own $200,000 in life insurance and a client has $100,000, you won't be afraid of the prospect. If you know the prospect needs more, you won't care if the prospect can or can't afford it. If you own $200,000 and move up to $300,000, you will start thinking a little bigger in terms of what he or she will suggest to prospects.

There is no greater proof of belief in the product than to purchase it in large quantities. Feldman frequently displayed his own program as an illustration. If the you does the same, this will show the prospect that you own the product, and that will increase the prospect's confidence in the life insurance and also in you as the agent.

If you believe that what you are doing is helping people help themselves, purchasing the policy on yourself reinforces that attitude. In your own mind, you have to buy it – and then you will be able to sell it. But if you don't buy it first, you will never sell it.

Sales Principle 9: Attitude

Feldman believed that your biggest asset is a positive attitude. If you decide you are going to feel wonderful, strong, and excited, then you have the power to move mountains. You can begin to get this feeling when you become convinced that through life insurance you can help another human being.

Feldman said that the most important person to disturb and get steamed up is yourself. Prospects know from the way you sit, the way you look at them, and in particular the way you say something, that you are certain about the advice you are giving. After all, what is enthusiasm except excitement in your voice? Feldman would say, "It's not what you say, but how you say it."

Speak slowly, clearly, softly, but definitely – and enthusiasm and sincerity will carry over.

Sales Principle 10: Ask Disturbing Questions

For Feldman, disturbing questions were powerful sales tools. Here are examples of some of Feldman's questions:

•   "What would you say if I told you I want 30% of everything you have in this world – and I want it now in cash?" This question forces prospects to face the fact that taxes will hit the estate once he or she is dead.

•   "Do you want your little boy to go to school? It isn't the policy that costs money. It's the education that costs money. May I talk to you about doing something about it? Which is cheaper, paying for your children's education in four years or 18 years? You have 18 years to pay for his education – if you begin now. You can't begin now? Then you'll have to pay for it all at once! Could you – right now – pay for his first year of college?"

•   "How much is your life worth?"

•   "People never die at the right time! What makes you think it will be different for you?" Disturbing questions are designed to cause the prospect to think and to bring emotion into the sales process.

Sales Principle 11: Preparation

Even when selling $100 millions of life insurance, Feldman still spent two hours each night studying and preparing for the following day. It's important to read and stay up on what's happening. It's important that you know what you are talking about.

You need to make life insurance simple and to stay away from things that confuse people. Here's Feldman's advice on that: Spend more time in preparation than in presentation, and never make a call until you are prepared. Feldman's study and preparation enabled him to make each sales call with confidence. He would prioritize most important things to be done for the next day. He would plan sales calls, service calls, and office work for the week.

Feldman's object in planning was to do what he knows he should do, and avoid doing what he knows he shouldn't do. That was his definition of self-discipline.

Sales Principle 12: Focus

An important characteristic that I somehow missed throughout the years I've read and listened to Feldman's materials was his exceptional focus. Feldman focused primarily on one market – privately held businesses that had issues with estate planning and business continuation.

I am particularly impressed with the importance of his packages and the way they bring focus and confidence to targeting a specific market.

Feldman was once asked at the MDRT annual meeting, "Since you are working the business market, do you do pension plans, sick-pay plans, or disability insurance?"

Feldman's answer was "No." He believed that people should be knowledgeable and know what they are doing. He told his audience he was going to continue to spend his time creating packages that create bundles of money to continue businesses.

Sales Principle 13: Power Phrases

Feldman believed that power phrases made a big difference in making a sale. And he developed and used some amazing such power phrases. Here are a few of his more effective power phrases:

• "You'll have the same problems when I walk out as you had when I walked in...unless you let me take your problems with me."

• "If you can't put away 3% of the amount now, where would 100% come from later? Buy a little less, but begin now."

• "How much is your life worth? How much did you insure it for?"

- "I sell discounted dollars. May I show you?"

- "Many people buy not because they believe, but because the salesperson believes."

- "Doing nothing doesn't solve your problem; it only postpones it. You have a right to postpone it. But if you postpone solving your problem, you know who will solve it? Your spouse."

Ben Feldman's Sales Principles

Ben Feldman is considered by many to be the greatest life insurance salesperson who ever lived, and for good reason. And fortunately for all of us, he was always willing to share with other agents the foundational principles of his sales success:

1. Making Calls
2. Packages
3. Don't Sell Life Insurance!
4. Simple Concepts
5. Discounted Dollars
6. Cash Value Life Insurance
7. Put Premiums Into Perspective
8. Sell Yourself
9. Attitude
10. Ask Disturbing Questions
11. Preparation
12. Focus
13. Power Phrases

For you looking to find your "personal best," it might be wise to integrate some of these principles that Ben Feldman utilized to become the best of the best.

Chapter 5

Joe Gandolfo

"People won't buy what you're selling just because it has a low price." – Joe Gandolfo Joe Gandolfo was born in Richmond, Kentucky, in 1936. His mother died of cancer when he was 13 years old, and his father died of a heart attack when Gandolfo was 17.

Gandolfo graduated from college in 1958 and played a summer of minor league baseball. In 1959, he was teaching when he was recruited into the life insurance business.

Gandolfo memorized a 22-page sales script before going to his company's training school. He could only sell $5,000 and $10,000 of Life Paid Up at 65. He thought having only two options helped him. It gave him a track to run on as well as focus. And he couldn't get mixed up.

Gandolfo started his sales career in Baton Rouge, Louisiana, where he knew no one. The company guaranteed him $450 a month if he could sell 10 policies or $100,000 in 90 days. He sold $92,000 in the first week.

After two years of setting company records, Gandolfo and his family moved to Lakeland, Florida. Not knowing anyone, he started calling on ministers. He then branched out by asking ministers for names of young couples. Funeral homes were his next market, and pharmacists were next. Then he called on personnel directors, sole proprietors, and executives who were new to the area. He focused on one occupation or market before moving onto the next.

Gandolfo's first goals were to earn his Chartered Life Underwriter (CLU) designation and to qualify for the Million Dollar Round Table. He achieved both in 1965, at age 29. Gandolfo then decided on another goal. He had heard about Ben Feldman, and he knew that Feldman sold more life insurance than two-thirds of the 1,800 life insurance companies.

Gandolfo realized that one of Feldman's secrets was that he concentrated exclusively on a single group, the principal owners of private businesses. They had assets that were not easily marketable and, without life insurance, they might have to liquidate their businesses to pay taxes.

In 1966, Gandolfo set a goal to beat Feldman and become the number one producer. He started working with higher income groups: ranchers, automobile dealers, physicians, and attorneys. By 1970, he passed Ben Feldman in volume. In 1971, he wrote $114 million. By 1974, he hit $500 million. In 1975, he sold $1 billion!!!

Beginning in 1985, Gandolfo focused exclusively on estate planning and tax-shelters. He charged a consulting fee and was booked 12 months in advance.

Gandolfo was a devout Catholic and attended mass every day. He believes the talents you possess are God's gifts to you, and what you do with those talents is your gift back to God.

Gandolfo gave 50% of his adjusted gross income to God, and some of it went to Christian ministries that feed the hungry worldwide, like Operation Blessing. Gandolfo passed away from cancer in February 2015. He sent me an email about 5 weeks before he passed. It said thanks for the kind words, referring to the book.

Even though it's been more than 30 years, I still can remember driving, listening to Gandolfo on cassette tapes as he talked about the importance of being right with the man upstairs. Gandolfo has authored and co-authored a number of books. Unfortunately, most are out of print, but you can occasionally find a used copy. They are gems!

His books include the following:
• Ideas Are a Dime a Dozen but the Man Who Puts Them into Practice Is Priceless
• God, I'll Give You All the Credit…And I'll take All the Commissions
• How to Sell Yourself without Selling Your Soul

- Sell & Grow Rich – The 10 Habits of Highly Successful Salespeople
- Selling is 98 Percent Understanding Human Beings… 2 Percent Product Knowledge

Gandolfo was influenced by Vince Lombardi, the legendary coach of the Green Bay Packers, who believed that a person's priorities should be in this order -- God, family, and job (for Lombardi, specifically the Green Bay Packers). One of the consistent themes in Gandolfo's books is that selling is 98% understanding human beings and 2% product knowledge. Unfortunately, I believe that we as a business have reversed that formula; we're spending 98% of our time on product knowledge and only 2% understanding human beings. Gandolfo uses a quote from Oliver Wendell Holmes, "Many ideas grow better when transplanted into another mind than in the one where they sprang up."

When you learn from Gandolfo, what you are getting is the product of a man who has read a lot of books, heard many people speak, and adopted what he could use into his own personality. I encourage you to take from Gandolfo the great ideas and fit them with your own individual personality.

Sales Principle 1: Attitude

Here are some of Gandolfo's thoughts on attitude:

• God gave you 24 hours each day. If you don't utilize them to the best of your ability, you deceive God, your family, and yourself.

• The ideas between your ears are the only things that make you different from the other salespeople.

• Gandolfo shares a quote from George Bernard Shaw on work habits: "People are always blaming their circumstances for what they are. I don't believe in circumstances. The people who get on in this world are the people who get up and look for the circumstances they want and if they can't find them, they make them."

• Gandolfo said the most influential book he's read is Think and Grow Rich by Napoleon Hill.

• Enthusiasm keeps us productive. Without it, your talents can be wasted. You won't have the drive to get out there and use your talents. Enthusiasm is the key ingredient of a successful person, no matter what business.

• To be enthusiastic, you need complete confidence in your product and belief it offers a benefit. You can't believe in it without owning it.

• Believe in the importance of enthusiasm, which means to be possessed by God.

Sales Principle 2: Sell Yourself

For Gandolfo, if what he was selling was so good for his prospect, then it was good for him. Gandolfo said he didn't fully appreciate the value of life insurance or begin to reach his goals until he owned large amounts of it.

Gandolfo believed that whatever you do, you can't do it effectively unless he or she believes in it. Before he owned a million dollars of insurance on his own life, he couldn't sell a million dollars on anyone else's life because he didn't see how anyone could afford it. Gandolfo believed that if you don't believe in the product enough to buy it, then you are lying to the prospect on every sales call.

Sales Principle 3: Goals

For Gandolfo, goals are critical. He believed that you have to know what you are working for, and you need goals to keep up a high level of enthusiasm.

When Gandolfo started out in the business, his goal was to make at least one sale a day – even if the sale was only a $5,000 or $10,000 policy. He then raised his goal to make two sales day. His quota would be 10 sales a week, 40 sales each month, and 480 policies for the year.

Gandolfo continued to increase his goals. Eventually, he beat Ben Feldman, with $100 million in sales, and achieved his goal. He then set his sights on a billion dollars in sales, which he reached in 1975.

Sales Principle 4: Planning and Imagining

Gandolfo's sales began to improve when he started using the technique of imagining. Before making a presentation, he would close his eyes and imagine the presentation, the questions and objections, his answers, and the successful close of the sale.

With planning and imagining, you know ahead of time how you will react during the sales call. You won't get caught off guard and stumble for an answer to an objection.

Positive reinforcement also comes along with effective imagining. The more the salesperson believes he or she can do something, the more likely it will happen. The mind is an incredible tool once a person learns how to use it.

By going through sales in the mind, you anticipate objections, and by imagining a sale in advance, the mind thinks positively, which a key ingredient to selling.

Sales Principle 5: Study

Gandolfo believed that, whatever you do, you should pick one area and become an expert in it. One way for the salesperson to become an expert is to read everything you can get your hands on – you should concentrate on information that relates to your specialty. Gandolfo would spend 20 hours a week studying and reading business-related material.

Sales Principle 6: Sales Approach

For Gandolfo, the key to getting appointments is to ask simple questions. For example, he would ask questions like this one: "Would you have any objection to reviewing your life insurance with me?"
For someone new in the business, Gandolfo suggests that you ask that question of every human being you meet.

Here's another simple approach Gandolfo used to get appointments. "I don't want to sell you anything now, but I want an opportunity to meet with you and share an idea that's been a help to other auto dealers (or whatever occupation is appropriate) here in Lincoln (or whatever city is appropriate). If it fits in with your philosophy and pocketbook, fine. If not, I'll be on my way."

Why does this approach work so well? It works for several good reasons.

First, the prospect is bound to be more interested in you sharing an idea rather than buying something. Who doesn't want to hear an idea? When it comes down to it, the only things the you as a life insurance producer have to sell are ideas. People buy the idea not the thing.

Second, everyone, no matter their occupation, believes their problems are unique. They will want to deal with a specialist. An auto dealer will respond especially positively when you say "the idea has been a help to other auto dealers, like yourself."

Third, Gandolfo encourages you to state the prospect's city because everyone likes dealing with someone who understands the local area. Gandolfo continues his sales approach by asking, "Would next Tuesday or Thursday be convenient?"

Remember, each prospect is thinking, "From eight to five, I'm making money. I don't want to take time from my making money to talk about this salesperson making money."

If the prospect won't give you an appointment, Gandolfo suggests that you ask, "May I ask you a question? When John Adams was president in the late-eighteenth and early-nineteenth centuries, the federal government came within three votes of abolishing the patent office. They thought they had invented everything that could be invented, so what was the use of having a patent office? Since then, we have had the telephone, car, television, airplanes, computers, smart phones, etc. So, Mr. Prospect, my question for you is, have you closed your patent office?

"If you owned a store, you would want the latest merchandise, no matter what business you're in. You probably would go to seminars or training for new ideas. Well, there are new ideas and concepts in life insurance.

"I have new ideas and concepts in life insurance. I have new ideas, and all I want to do is run them past you. If they fit with your philosophy and pocketbook, fine. If not, I'll be on my way. Do you have an objection?"

I tell you emphatically, this sales approach WORKS!

Sales Principle 7: Presentation

Gandolfo started his presentation with an introduction. The purpose of the introduction is to establish the producer's credibility. Gandolfo would use it to explain why the prospect should do business with him instead of someone else.

Gandolfo would point out on his business card that he was a life member of the MDRT. (Early in his career, he would say, "I'm on schedule to qualify for the MDRT.) He would talk about the National Quality Award, which he received because he stays in touch with his clients. Then he would point out that he is a Chartered Life Underwriter, which he would describe as being an equivalent in the life insurance business as a CPA is in accounting.

Next, Gandolfo would find out what the prospect needs with a series of thought-provoking, open-ended questions:

- "How do you feel about life insurance as an investment?"

- "What's your philosophy on life insurance?"

- "How do you feel about spouse insurance?"

• "Do you prefer permanent or term insurance?" (Gandolfo's approach was that, if the client wanted term insurance, he'd sell term insurance. The following year, after the client loves him, he'd be back to sell "permanent term." He believed that the agent should not try to change the prospect's philosophy at first).

• "What would happen if you die or become disabled?" (Gandolfo used this question to establish the need for life insurance and income protection.)

• "What will happen if you retire and live a long life?" (This question would lead to a discussion of permanent insurance and long-term cash values).

Gandolfo believed the key to a good presentation is good open-ended questions. The key to understanding people is asking questions, and asking tons of them. Asking those questions gets the prospect talking about the prospect, and that will give you clues about what they will buy.

The secret to a good salesperson is the combined ability to ask good questions to listen closely to the answers. Gandolfo liked to say that God gave us two ears and one mouth; He wants you to do twice as much listening as talking. No one ever learns from talking.
Your job is to guide the prospect with the right questions so that he or she comes to the conclusion that he or she should buy.

Sales Principle 8: Closing

When it came time to close, Gandolfo would go through the policy illustration and answer the prospect's questions about what happens to the money should the prospect do any of these four things:
- Die
- Become disabled
- Quit
- Retire

Then Gandolfo would give the prospect options. And in doing so, he would avoid "yes or no" options. For example, you never want to say, "Do you want to buy this policy?"

Instead, Gandolfo stressed, you want to give "yes or yes" options. For example, assume that a $100,000 policy will cost $2,000 a year, while a $200,000 will cost $4,000 a year. That being the case, you would then ask the prospect, "Which one best fits with your present financial situation?"

In closing, objections of course often arise. The key to handling objections, according to Gandolfo, is you should address them in the presentation. If you keep hearing the same objections, then you should change the presentation to answer it.

Here are Gandolfo's approaches to the common objections, "I want to think it over" and "I can't afford it."

"I want to think it over." -- With this objection, prospect is saying, "I don't know you well enough. You haven't explained it clearly to me, or you've gone so fast that I haven't been able to comprehend it."

First, Gandolfo says, don't take tomorrow for an answer – lots of prospects say "I want to think it over." If they think it over, 95% don't buy. Callbacks don't pay off.

If presenting correctly, you are finding out what the prospect wants and satisfying those wants. What could possibly happen in a few days to make him want to buy, if he doesn't want it buy it now?

The question the agent should ask with regard to this objection is, "What additional information do you hope to learn to make a decision?" By asking that question, you are telling the prospect that waiting won't help him make a more informed decision.

Gandolfo says that you can also point out that successful people make decisions while relevant information is still fresh in their minds.

A follow-up question for the prospect who wants to think it over might be: "Whatever you do, buy or not buy, you're making a decision today. Does it make sense to expose your family to death or illness when you could protect them for X amount of dollars that you really won't miss?"

"I can't afford it." – Gandolfo says that one way to address this objection is to get a money commitment early in the presentation. If you haven't done that, then he or she might ask the question, "Would spending the money make a difference in your lifestyle?"

Another good question to combat this objection, Gandolfo says, is, "What amount do you feel you could set aside?" Then you can lower the benefit to match premium. In other words, offer a lower-priced alternative. Another approach Gandolfo recommends is to ask, "May I ask you a question? Why did you allow this interview? Why did you allow me to come in here if you couldn't afford it? Now what is the real reason?"

Sales Principle 9: Referred Leads

Agents are always asking for leads. But Gandolfo believed that referred leads are the best leads, and they are free.

Gandolfo learned about referred leads from a paint salesman. He went to the salesman's apartment and saw all of the salesman's awards for being the top paint salesman in the United States.

Gandolfo asked him how he did it. The paint salesman said he used the magic words, "I need your help." Then he would ask for three names.

Think about it! Who says "No" when you say "I need your help"?

Notice that he asked for three names, not five or ten. People think in threes. There aren't many people with more than three good friends.

Gandolfo started telling everyone, "I need your help," and asking for three names. It didn't make any difference if he had sold the people he asked or not.

Gandolfo would follow his request by saying, "I will approach them on the same professional basis that I approached you."

Gandolfo would find out as much as possible about the referrals – age, occupation, etc. Then he asked, "Will you see them before next week? If so, would you mind mentioning my name? And would you mind if I mentioned your name?"

Then when he called, he would ask, "Did 'Sam Jones' mention my name?"

Sales Principle 10: Product Knowledge

Remember, Gandolfo didn't sell life insurance, he sold ideas. The top producers sell concepts and ideas, not products.
Gandolfo believed that selling is 98% understanding human beings and 2% product knowledge. It is important to know the product, but knowing everything about the product doesn't mean the agent has to tell everything to every client on every sales call. Too many technical details confuse prospects.

Gandolfo knew that customers don't want to know how an air conditioner works, they just want to know it will keep them cool on a hot day. You have to listen to prospects tell what they want to buy. The good salesperson uses product knowledge to make appropriate recommendations that meet the prospect's needs and close the sale.

Sales Principle 11: Advice for Beginners

Gandolfo had two important pieces of sales advice for the beginning salesperson:
1. Ask everyone the following question: "Would you have any objections to reviewing your life insurance with me?"

2. Pick an area you understand, and become an expert in it.

Sales Principle 12: See Lots of People – Make Calls

The president of a life insurance company used to tell people that Gandolfo had 16 years of experience, even though he had only been in the business for eight years. At first Gandolfo was confused by that, but he said that when he thought about it, it made a lot of sense to him. "If I see 500 people and you see 250 people, regardless of age or number of years in the business, I have twice the experience because I've talked to twice as many people."

Gandolfo said, "I can't impress enough upon you who are starting in the business – to see the people. By virtue of seeing people, getting objections, getting the "no's" and getting the "yes's". You are sharpening your sales skills. Each no gets you closer to a yes – you learn from the no's."

Joe Gandolfo's Sales Principles

Joe Gandolfo was a record-setting salesperson who spent his career setting lofty goals and smashing them. And like so many of the greats, he was always willing to share his principles with others in the business. For Gandolfo, these principles are the foundation for being the best you can be:

1. Attitude
2. Sell Yourself
3. Goals
4. Planning and Imagining
5. Study
6. Sales Approach
7. Presentation
8. Closing
9. Referred Leads
10. Product Knowledge
11. Advice for Beginners
12. See Lots of People – Make Calls

Remember that he believed the talents you possess are God's gifts to you, and what you do with those talents is your gift back to God. For the agent with a more spiritual nature, and for those who simply want to get the best from themselves, Gandolfo's principles are good ones to follow.

THE COMMON DENOMINATORS

Albert E. N. Gray gave a speech at the 1940 annual convention of the National Association of Life Underwriters (NALU), which is now the National Association of Insurance and Financial Advisors (NAIFA). Gray had more than 30 years of sales, sales management, and home office experience when he gave his speech, "The Common Denominator of Success."

Gray said that he was supervising salespeople without understanding why some were successful and others failed. He began looking for the common denominators of success. Gray determined that the secret of success is that the successful salesperson formed the habit of doing what failures don't do.

Gray's conclusion is just as true as it sounds and as simple as it seems. The things that successful people don't like to do are the very same things you, I, and all other human beings don't like to do. But the successful people have the discipline to do those things.

What are the common denominators that made Frank Bettger, W. Clement Stone, Ben Feldman, and Joe Gandolfo so successful? What did they do that the failures didn't do?

Common Denominator 1: Enthusiasm

Bettger, Stone, Feldman, and Gandolfo all understood the importance of enthusiasm in their success.

For Bettger, enthusiasm saved his career. For Stone, enthusiasm was the most important factor in selling. For Feldman, enthusiasm was the excitement in the salesperson's voice. He strongly believed that it's not what you say but how you say it. For Gandolfo, enthusiasm is the key ingredient of a successful person, no matter what business.

Bettger mentioned that he had seen individuals with great technical expertise fail because of their lack of enthusiasm, while people with less than half as much technical knowledge succeeded because of their enthusiasm. Think about it!

Any listener who has been in business for more than a few years and has seen salespeople come and go will almost certainly agree with Bettger's statement.

Enthusiasm is also contagious. It picks up the people around you. Enthusiasm affects your prospect.

Do you believe being enthusiastic improves your chances of a sale? If you are a wholesaler, do you believe brokers prefer working with someone who is enthusiastic?

I spend a lot of time observing presentations, and pay close attention to presenters. I remember once, the first presenter at a seminar had great technical material but was anything but enthusiastic. Everyone in the audience was bored. The next presenter had little substance but was extremely enthusiastic. The audience loved her. Why? Because of her enthusiasm. If the audience had to choose a person with which to do business, and these two presenters were the options, which do you think they would have chosen?

Bettger and Stone both emphasized the point that feelings follow action. If you want to be enthusiastic, all you have to do is act enthusiastic. Does that sound hokey to you? It may be hokey, but it works! Are you more concerned with hokey or with results? Associate with enthusiastic people, and remember that enthusiasm is contagious.

In our high-tech age, very few people talk about the importance of enthusiasm. That's actually great news, because if the you understand the importance of enthusiasm, it makes it easier to stand out from all of those producers who don't.

Common Denominator 2: Make Calls, and See the People

Technology may change; the way producers prospect may change; the way producers see and meet with people may change; but the fact that you need to make calls hasn't changed.

Bettger turned his career around when he listened to the president of Fidelity Mutual, who said, "This business narrows down to one thing -- seeing the people." Bettger believed him and sold more business in the following ten weeks than he had sold in the previous ten months.

Stone's sales system was business-to-business, door-to-door. Sales reps were expected to make 20 presentations and sell 20 policies a day. That does not happen if the rep doesn't make calls.

Feldman said, "There is no easy way -- you have to make calls! Nothing happens until you make a call."

Gandolfo said, "I can't impress on you enough to see the people. By virtue of seeing people, getting objections, getting no's and yesses,' you sharpen your sales skills! Each no gets you closer to a yes. You learn from the nos."

The president of the life insurance company understood the reason for Gandolfo's success when he told Gandolfo that he had 16 years of experience when he was only in the business for 8 years. It was because he made twice as many calls as most salespeople.

Our business is really simple. It's a numbers game. If you track calls and sales, you know that there is a certain number of calls you need to make to make a sale. Does that sound easy? What salesperson enjoys keeping any kind of record? Personally, I hate it! Every salesperson I know hates keeping records.

Remember the successes do the things the failures don't like keeping track of calls. There are some programs today that make it much easier to track calls. It still requires discipline to do it, but once you start, it grow into a habit, it becomes easy.

Bettger actually found it liberating to track calls, interviews, and commissions. He knew exactly what each call was worth. Did that help him to make more calls? Definitely, because he knew that every time he made a call he was earning x amount. If you knew that every time you made a call it was worth $250. That would be great motivation to make an extra call.

There is a little poem that I learned early in my career:

> What's behind the door?
> I cannot tell,
> But this I know,

And know it well,
The more I open,
The more I sell.

It's been over 100 years since Bettger heard, "The insurance business narrows down to one thing -- seeing the people."
The principle is still the same; it has not changed over the past 100 years. If you want to succeed, you have to make the calls.

Common Denominator 3: Planning and Study

Both planning and study are so important that I would like to look at them separately.

First, let's consider planning. Early in my career, someone told me that the secret to success in our business is simple -- plan your work and work your plan. That sounds so simple and so easy. And that's exactly what Bettger, Stone, Feldman, and Gandolfo did throughout their careers.

Bettger set aside Saturday mornings to plan his next week. He knew exactly who he was going to call and what he was going to say. He then could relax the remainder of the weekend. As a result, he was ready on Monday and made his calls with confidence. He also spent 30 minutes planning his calls each morning.

Stone believed that one of the most important habits the salesperson can develop happens at the end of each day – planning the following day's activity. He did his planning at home in the evening, away from the distractions of the office. Stone taught the importance of planning to his executive team.

Feldman would spend from two to three hours in the evening studying and planning. He stated his objective in planning was to schedule what he knew he should do and to avoid doing what he shouldn't do. He would plan his calls for the following day. For many of his calls, he reviewed Dun & Bradstreet Reports. He knew financial information about the business before he called on the business.

Gandolfo not only planned his calls, he also used visualization techniques prior to making calls. He would see himself walking into the office, making the presentation, answering objections, and closing the sale.

My guess is that all four of these sales greats used visualization in some form. I remember listening to a recording of Napoleon Hill talking about teaching visualization to Stone's managers and sales reps.

Planning requires discipline and commitment. I get a lot more done when I plan my day the night before. If you really want to see a difference, take 30 minutes on a Sunday and plan for Monday.

Does it make a difference? Yes!!! The salesperson who plans well is prepared mentally and his or her productivity increases.

Now, let's consider study. There is only one way to grow personally and professionally, and that's by setting aside specific time to study. Betgger spent 30 minutes each morning studying. For Stone, his planning and study time was in the evening. Gandolfo spent 20 hours a week studying, and always had study material with him.

One of the best times to study and learn is while you are driving. I can still remember listening to Stone, Feldman, and Gandolfo on cassette tape with a cassette recorder plugged into my car's lighter. Believe it or not, at the time that was considered high tech.

It's much easier today with CDs and MP3s, and there is tremendous material that you can access. I still listen while driving today. Right now, I am listening to Brian Tracy on self-discipline.

Part of the reason Stone, Feldman, and Gandolfo are such a strong part of my sales thinking is that I have listened to them many times. When you only listen once, you will miss ideas. Learning is all about repetition and when you listen frequently the ideas become part of you.

Repetition is so important in self-improvement. Think about this! You listen to a song once – you may remember some of the words. You listen 5 times, you can remember the words with music in the background. You listen 10 times, you can sing without the music. Salespeople will complain about repetition but repetition leads to mastery.

I want to add a thought about preparation and have a question for you, "Have you ever really practiced your presentation?"

Bettger's sales increased when an agent moved into his area from Georgia. The agent suggested that they practice their presentations on one another. Both improved their presentations and sales as a result.

Stone's sales reps practiced their presentation on each other.

When Ben Feldman was developing a new package, he would test and practice on his wife, kids, and office staff.

If you want to improve your results, find someone who will give honest feedback on your presentation. Observe the presentations of others, and continuously look for ideas to improve your presentation.

I want to close this section with a quote from Larry Wilson. Wilson did a lot of training in the life insurance business. He defined insurance professionals as having three qualities, "They're good and they know it. They keep getting better, and they critique their own performance."

For wholesalers, here's my one rant on webinars: Ninety percent of webinars we do as an industry are a waste of time. Too many webinars are totally focused on product. Successful agents and brokers want sales ideas and concepts to go with product information.

There are too many webinars. It's better to do one effective webinar than 10 ineffective webinars.

Too often we confuse activity with results. There is tendency is to look at webinars as an end in themselves. We need to ask ourselves, are they effective? Are the webinars resulting in sales?

Many of the Webinar attendees tend to be like students of the business, who sell very little. The brokers that wholesalers really want to reach don't attend because they are spending their time more productively.

Here are a few suggestions for those wholesalers giving presentations:

First, understand your audience. With a life presentation, you should present differently for life producers than you would if you were introducing a life product to Medicare Supplement agents.

Second, have a clear objective concerning what you want to accomplish. Ask yourself, what is the one key idea that you want attendees to walk away with?

Third, use polling questions or chat feature to measure engagement. If you have thirty attendees and there are only two responses to questions, your audience is not engaged.
And finally, include a sales idea or sales concept that will help agents and brokers sell the product.

Common Denominator 4: Focus on One Product or Market

All four of the sales greats we've been discussing were focused on specific markets or specific product. As his career evolved, Bettger focused almost exclusively on the business market. Stone focused on the sale of one kind of policy, a pre-issue accident plan. Later as his company introduced new plans, the company developed new sales teams to sell specific plans. Stone believed that the secret to his and his salespeople's success was that their efforts were concentrated on the sale of one policy. Feldman focused on the owners of close privately held corporations. He sold packages. His packages were bundles of whole life designed to solve a specific problem.

Gandolfo focused on specific occupations, like ministers, funeral home directors, and pharmacists. Before moving to tax and estate planning, he focused exclusively on working with automobile dealers around the United States.

I was thinking about Gandolfo's comment starting sales after going through his initial training, he could only sell $5,000 and $10,000 life paid up at 65. He said this kept it simple and kept him from getting confused. Gandolfo advised, "Find one area and become an expert in that area, and your confidence will grow." Years ago, the company I was working with did business with an organization, National Teacher Associates (NTA). The president of NTA learned the business from Stone at Combined. NTA focused on selling cancer plans to teachers -- one product, one market. I had the privilege of attending NTA's new-agent training class. I was the first home-office person who attended the class.

The training was based on Stone's success principles. The class was five and one-half days long. When the agent left the class, the agent was an expert in the sale of cancer insurance. The agent knew the words to open a discussion, present the product, answer the objections, and close the sale. Each agent had written out the presentation and practiced. There was no confusion and sales rep was confident as a result.

One thing that I remember from my early days in the business is that there were some small Life insurance companies that had better agent retention rates than some larger companies the larger companies had more extensive training and financing programs. The difference was that the smaller companies focused on one product.

It makes me think about Franklin Life Insurance Company years ago. Franklin Life's ads in the life insurance industry publications focused on agents who had failed with other life insurance companies and then succeeded with Franklin Life. The ads actually showed the agents income before and after joining Franklin Life.

Why were those agents successful with Franklin Life after failing with another company? With Franklin Life, they focused on one plan -- The President's Plan -- and they were experts on the one plan.

When you focus on one product or market, you become an expert. As a result, your confidence grows.

While writing this section, I keep thinking about Bum Phillips, when he coached the Houston Oilers. The reporters were on him because the Oilers didn't have as many play variations as some other teams. His response was, it's difficult to be aggressive when you're confused.

I also thought about my friend, Irwin Cohen. Irwin has presented at the MDRT Annual Meeting several times, and he is one of the leaders in the United States in disability insurance sales. In his presentation, Irwin shares his struggles in the business until he focused. Today, he is focused on one product in one market, disability insurance to attorneys. One of the reasons for Irwin's success is his focus.

I remember talking with Ben Feldman's son, Marvin, who is a great salesperson himself. I asked Marvin what advice he has for agents, especially new agents. Marvin said that after you have learned the basics, you should pick a market and specialize in it. Marvin said the producer should form alliances with agents who are experts in the other products and markets. Marvin has focused on estate planning and business continuation. He doesn't do group, health, long term care or disability income. He formed alliances with experts in those areas.

Common Denominator 5: Sell Yourself – Make the Most Important Sale First

How can you sell something you don't believe in enough to buy yourself? How can you overcome the objection, "I can't afford it," if the you feel the same way?

Bettger owned a $1,000 policy on himself. Then he purchased a $25,000 policy. The next year, he jumped in the company standings from 92nd to 13th. He no longer feared the objection, "I can't afford it."

Feldman said you have to buy it first. If the producer doesn't buy it, he said, the producer will never sell it. When Feldman was on the debit and owned a $500 policy, he sold $500 policies. As he increased his personal life insurance, he sold larger policies.
Gandolfo said that if life insurance is so good for the prospect, then it's good for you too. You can't do anything effectively until you believe in it. Gandolfo began to reach his goals when he began to own large amounts of life insurance.

When you believe in life insurance enough to buy significant amounts yourself, it comes through in every presentation. Prospects are influenced by your belief.

The concept is so simple, yet so hard. My question for you is, do you believe in what you are selling enough to buy it on yourself?

Common Denominator 6: Questions

Questions were an important part of Bettger's, Stone's, Feldman's, and Gandolfo's presentations. They all used questions effectively.

Several years ago, I was doing a training presentation in Chicago. Someone asked me where I learned to sell. I said Socrates. I told him – I may be old but not old enough to have known him personally.

Socrates approach was rather than argue, use questions to change the other person's thinking.

What does a good attorney and a good salesperson have in common? Answer: They only ask questions when they know how the witness or prospect will answer.

Every trial lawyer and salesperson can thank Socrates.

People hate to be sold, but they love to buy. What's the secret? Answer: Questions!

Bettger and Stone were believers in the Socratic approach.

To illustrate, I'll share the 4 questions used in presenting Critical Illness protection:

1.   "Who do you know who has been diagnosed with cancer, had a heart attack, or had a stroke?" Everyone knows someone who has suffered one of these conditions. They automatically think of the person closest to them. As a result, they become emotionally involved in the sales process.

2.   "Was it expected?" The answer is "no." No one expects to have one of those conditions. This demonstrates the randomness of a critical illness.

3.   "Was there unplanned financial or emotional stress on the family or business?" The answer is "yes." Ninety-nine percent of the time, there is financial stress that accompanies one of these conditions; one hundred percent of the time there is emotional stress.

4.   "Would cash have helped?" The answer is "yes." Most prospects will tell you how the person would have used the cash, and by doing so they will have given the salesperson a reason they themselves will buy.

These four questions demonstrate the need for critical illness.

Remember, people buy because of emotion, and then look for logic to justify their decision.

I had a friend who was trying to close a life insurance case to fund a buy-sell agreement. The two partners just kept putting him off, even though he gave every logical reason for them to buy and buy immediately. He was finally able to close the sale.

He asked one of the partners these two questions:

"How would you like to be in business with your partner's widow?"

"If your partner died, how would you talk with his widow about setting a price on her interest in the business?"

There is another thing that good questions do. If you are making statements, the customer is thinking either about you or the product you are selling. If you are asking questions, the prospect is thinking about himself or herself. In answering questions, the prospect gets more involved and stays involved.
Bettger was about to sell a New York manufacturer because of his questions. With his questions, he was able to determine the manufacturer's major concern. Remember, the manufacturer already had ten proposals. Why did Bettger get the sale? His questions helped the manufacture identify his concern. Everyone else was just selling product.

Gandolfo's presentation was based on series of open-ended questions to determine the prospect's needs and philosophy of life insurance. If you ask good open-ended questions, the prospect will tell you what he or she wants and the reasons he or she will buy. But you have to listen to the prospect's answers. Include a couple of Gandolfo's questions

Ben Feldman was the master of the disturbing question. His questions were designed to help the prospect see that the prospect had a problem.

Think about Feldman's questions:

- "How much is your life worth?"
- "People never die at the right time. What makes you think it will be different for you?"
- "How would your family get money out of the business if you didn't come back tomorrow?"

How do you become effective using questions in selling? You start asking questions! That's the only way to do it. Take some of the questions in this book and start using them.

Common Denominator 7: Stop selling insurance! Start selling what it does!

It's not about the product. It's about what the product does.

Remember our discussion about the drill. No one wants to buy a drill. They had a problem. They need a hole. The only reason they buy a drill to solve the problem.

Likewise, no one wants to buy insurance. Instead, they are worried about how can they buy groceries and pay their mortgage if they are sick or hurt and can't work. They have a problem. Income protection solves that problem.

If you only remember one thing from this audiobook, it's that We don't sell products, we solve problems. The product is simply the way we solve the problem.

Ben Feldman is considered to be the greatest life insurance salesman ever. And he didn't sell life insurance. His packages were all about solving a specific problem. Whole life was the solution to the problem.

Gandolfo and Bettger designed their questions to identify their prospect's problem.

When you look at what we do as solving problems, it can totally change your attitude. Years ago, a friend of mine has a client who was an auditor. The auditor mentioned that he needed to earn some additional income. The auditor was such an introvert; he couldn't lead a group in silent prayer.

My friend asked the auditor his thoughts on mutual funds.

The auditor said after life insurance needs are met and person has emergency fund, mutual funds are all right. You're betting on US economy, which is a good bet.

My friend said that his company was putting on some part-time people. Would you be interested? The auditor said I couldn't sell.

My friend said forget sell. Could you show people how to balance their budgets? If they need life insurance, could you suggest they buy more life insurance? And if there's anything left over, could you suggest the put it into a mutual fund?

The idea of selling was unacceptable to the auditor, but he could help others solve their financial problems.

That happened a long time ago but the last I heard the auditor was making more money part-time solving problems with life insurance and mutual funds than he was as an auditor.

One of the most powerful ways to drive home what insurance does are stories. Bettger used stories to demonstrate what life insurance does. Early in my career, I met a salesperson who used an Elba Communicator. The Elba Communicator was a briefcase with a screen, and it had a cassette recorder with film strips. There were a variety of specific presentations for retirement, family needs, spouse insurance, and income protection. The presentations were real life stories. There is nothing more powerful than a real-life story about what insurance does. This agent had a high closing rate. All he did was show the film that related to the prospect's problem. The film showed how insurance would solve a problem for the prospect. The Life Insurance Foundation for Education (LIFE) has some great stories and videos that you can use for this very purpose. Just go to the LIFE Website -- http://www.lifehappens.org/.

Bettger stated in one of his books, the greatest salesperson ever used stories. They called them parables.

What happens when you focus on product? Usually, you bore the prospect. Ever see a prospect's eyes start to glaze over?

When you focus on product, the prospect focuses on product. The prospect will ask product questions about the product and, in most cases, will not buy.

I remember a survey years ago about non-purchasers of disability income. These were individuals to whom an agent presented disability insurance and then the prospects did not buy. One of the main reasons they didn't buy was that the agent focused on the product and the prospect became confused.

My friend Keith Leech and I were discussing this issue of agents and advisors focused on product. Keith is the premier sales expert on critical illness and income protection in Canada. He told me about a recent meeting where four advisors came up to ask him questions. Three of the four were asking product questions. It was obvious those three understood the product much more than the fourth. The three hadn't been able to sell any critical illness and the fourth was hitting it out of the park with sales. The reason is simple. The three were selling the product and the fourth was selling what the product does.

In Closing

Early in my career, I was fortunate to meet Jack Wardlaw. Jack was the top sales person with Philadelphia Life. He was a sales master. He wrote a book, Top secrets of selling – Thought plus Action. I first read it many many years ago. The book was written in the1960's and it's been out of print, but I was able to find a copy.

Jack said, I have come to the conclusion that basic sales principles will remain unblemished from the time Grant Taggart sold his first policy till long after Ben Feldman sells his last. You can take a good salesman from any period, if they are vested with principles of good salesmanship and knowledge of current products and they would be successful today. Grant Taggart sold his first policy in 1914, riding to his appointment on horseback.
Jack wrote that over 45 years ago. The reason for Jack's great success was – he understood principles.
I would add competent with tools of technology.

It is time to focus on sales and success principles.

I love the way Frank Bettger closes How I Raised Myself from Failure to Success in Selling.

Bettger writes, and I completely agree, that you can do one of three things after reading to this book.

First, you can do nothing. If you do nothing, this book has been a waste of your time.

Second, you can say to yourself, "There are a lot of good ideas in this book. I'll try all of them. I'll give it a shot."

If you take either of those approaches, nothing will change. In fact, I will guarantee you that nothing will change. I know that from personal experience.

Third, though, you can say to yourself, "I'll pick four key concepts that I believe will have the greatest impact on me and my business, and I will commit to making them a part of me."

I would strongly support that kind of approach! Commit to implementing one idea for two weeks. Then move to idea number two, and so on.

I would to hear from you. My email is Ken@kensmithsales.com

All the best

Made in the USA
Columbia, SC
24 August 2017